Lessons From The Purple Tree

Briona,

Thanks so much for your support & caring.

God Bless,

Linda
2004

Copyright © 2004 Linda F. Felker, Ph.D.

ISBN 1-59113-515-X

All rights reserved. No part of this publication may be reproduced, stored in a retrieval system, or transmitted in any form or by any means, electronic, mechanical, recording or otherwise, without the prior written permission of the author.

Printed in the United States of America.

Booklocker.com, Inc.
2004

Lessons From The Purple Tree

Linda F. Felker, Ph.D.

This book is dedicated to
my husband, David Felker, for his
unwavering love and support, and to my mother, Mary
Ruth Fox, for her inspiration and faith.

About the Author

Linda F. Felker, Ph.D., has influenced the corporate world as a Management Development Consultant, Leadership Trainer, and Keynote Speaker for over 20 years. A member of The American Society of Training and Development, Dr. Felker holds a charter certification to administer the Myers Briggs Psychological Type Indicator.

She regularly volunteers her time with local organizations, and provides individual as well as group counseling and training sessions. Dr. Felker has been the guest speaker at International Conferences across America, and shared her knowledge and expertise in the field of Employee Training and Development, as well as Management Strategies for Employee Retention and Satisfaction.

Dr. Felker earned a Bachelor of Science degree and a Masters of Business Administration, with honors. She graduated *summe cum laude* with a Ph.D. in Human Resource Management, accompanied by studies in Family and Career Counseling.

Linda lives in Winston-Salem, NC with her husband David. She has three children and two grandchildren, and is a charter member of Grace Baptist Temple, where she is a member of the Adult Choir.

Table of Contents

Introduction xi

Trust 1

Vision, Mission, and Goals 9

Communication 15

Feedback 21

Commitment 27

The Leadership Challenge 37

Acknowledgements 45

References 47

Introduction

Mary Ruth Fox is an extraordinary artist. With what appears to be very little effort, she creates original, true-to-life oil paintings that are so realistic you can actually "feel" them. Her talent is God-given, and she uses this ability to touch the lives of others.

Mary Ruth is gracious and gentle, and works tirelessly and patiently to use her skill to the fullest, yet she seeks no recognition. She has a kind, generous nature. Best of all, Mary Ruth is my Mother.

My sister Sue inherited mother's artistic talent and ability. I did not.

I was four years, and Sue was six. My sister and I were sitting in straight-back chairs around the kitchen table working diligently in our coloring books. Sue was precise, and in control as she chose the right colors to complete her masterpiece. Sue even embellished her picture by using a pencil to draw a fence around the house and put additional flowers on her page. Each swipe of her crayon was perfection, and she always colored within the lines.

Even at four years old, I knew I could not color as well as my sister. I would never be able to draw and color, like

Sue, and certainly never come close to being artistic like my mother. My sister Sue had all the talent!

That particular day, my mother was standing at the kitchen stove, cooking dinner, and Sue said, "Hey mama, come look at my picture. I added a fence around the house, and drew in a few flowers to make it prettier."

Mother wiped her hands on a towel, and then stepped over to the table. She looked at Sue's color page, and said, "This is absolutely beautiful, Sue. I really like the way you added depth to your picture with the fence."

I sat there silently, and did not offer my color page to mother because I did not want her to see that my picture was not pretty like Sue's picture. I just could not color as well as Sue did, and I felt that I would never be able to measure up to Sue's artistic ability.

I would never be part of what they had in common. In my mind, I felt like my color page was ugly, and I started to crumple it up to throw it into the trash can.

Before I could do that, Sue said, "Hey Mama, look at what Linda did to her picture! She colored her tree PURPLE!"

I felt like sliding out of my chair and under the kitchen table because I did not want to disappoint my mother when she saw my coloring page. She would never be proud of it the way she was of Sue's picture.

Mother walked around the table, and picked up my paper. She studied it carefully for a moment, then said, "Linda, I love this picture. It shows true originality."

My sister laughed aloud, and said, "But mama, she colored the tree PURPLE! Everyone knows trees are green."

The next words my mother said to me are forever inscribed in my memory. She said, "Linda, this is *your* tree. You can color it any color you want to."

Lessons From The Purple Tree

As I sat there dejectedly staring at the floor, my mother continued. "You could have used the green crayon for your tree, and that would have been good. But you chose the purple crayon, and created something unique and individual to you. All the colors are beautiful. It is YOUR TREE. Color it any color you want."

"But mama", I cried. "Sue laughed at my picture. How could it be good like you said?" Mother cupped my face in her hands, and gently replied, "Linda, for the rest of your life there will be people who may not like what you create, or agree with what you do. You must decide what's best for you to do, and then do your very best with it."

"Just like you chose to color the tree purple, you will make choices that will decide the direction of your life. As long as your choices are based on doing the right thing and not hurting someone else, then your life will be full of bright colors, and purple trees."

I will never forget how proud I felt at that moment. And, I will always remember the greater lesson I learned that day about the colors of the world. My mother thought she was offering encouraging words to me regarding my coloring page. What she actually gave me was a far great gift.

She gave me the inspiration to be myself, the desire to help others, and the belief that using my own talents and gifts would help me accomplish my life goals.

Of course, at four years old, I did not comprehend the enormity of my mother's words at the kitchen table when she talked about my purple tree. As I grew older, I began to see the full outreach of what she said. As an adult, and as a professional, I value those words even more and the lessons they teach.

Trust is the first lesson gained from my purple tree and my mother's comforting words. Nothing of value can be successfully built, maintained, or enhanced without a solid foundation of Trust and Respect.

Trust is at the core of interpersonal relationships, as well as corporate structure. It takes a true leader to build a foundation of trust that can withstand today's corporate environment.

The next lesson from the Purple Tree is the importance of Vision, Mission, and Goals. Through her words and consistently strong example, my mother taught me that a life without purpose is full of missed opportunities and unfulfilled dreams.

The Purple Tree was born out of a four-year-old's vision of color. Once created, it was a reflection of the inner imaginings of a child, transferred to paper for all to see.

Leaders must establish and make decisions based on the overall goal of the organization. The corporate vision must be so clear that employees can see and understand it, and thereby comprehend their role within the company, and perform accordingly.

Strong leadership skill is essential to ensure the corporate mission is clear, vivid, and full of color to everyone in the company. Without an intense understanding of "why we do the work we do", the company may not be able to sustain even marginal success in today's world of tremendous competition and continuous change.

People who share a common sense of purpose can get where they are going quicker and easier, and will positively impact others who share the same goals.

The third lesson from The Purple Tree is Communication. My mother appropriately communicated with me on a level that I could understand and digest. She spoke the right words, at the right time, for the right reason, and to the right person. Her method of communicating was powerful enough to instill a lifelong desire for success into the mind of a child.

Leaders must communicate well in order to drive that intensive degree of desire and acceptance into the workforce.

Feedback is the fourth lesson from The Purple Tree. Mother knew how to give feedback, and never hesitated to offer it to any of her children. Mom's feedback was immediate. She did not put off giving necessary feedback, although, at times, it was difficult. She felt that children would not understand the message if she waited until 'later' to discuss the issue.

And, her feedback was balanced. She always spoke about what I was doing *right* as well as what needed changing or improving. Feedback from my mother was motivating and encouraging, as well as corrective.

There is a tremendously valuable lesson for the corporate world relating to providing employee feedback. Mother's methods were quite simple, but enormously successful.

The fifth lesson is Commitment. Without commitment, my mother would not have been able
to instill the values, principles, and legacy of superior performance in her children and family. Her dedication and enthusiasm in creating an inclusive environment, and providing encouragement to others, resulted in a lasting commitment from those whose lives she touched.

These five lessons are very simple concepts, yet many leaders struggle to accept and implement them into their work and personal lives. It takes dedication, time, and energy, but the rewards and benefits are worth the effort.

When an organization masters all five of these principles, they will reap solid benefits. The company and the employees will benefit from increased career and

Linda F. Felker, Ph.D.

business opportunities, higher, more efficient productivity, greater job satisfaction, higher work quality, and reduced stress.

Trust

As a child, I was very afraid of heights. The result of that fear was that I missed out on many fun adventures. I was so afraid of high places that I even refused to ride downhill on a sled, or go down a sliding board at the playground.

One of my earliest remembrances is of a vacation trip to visit family in West Jefferson County, North Carolina. This mountainous section of the country is incredibly beautiful, and many of my mother's relatives lived on farms surrounded by hills and valleys.

My sister was not afraid of the high mountains, and merrily played on the hillside with total abandon. One day, while visiting relatives who lived at the bottom of a mountain, Sue convinced me to follow her up the hill to watch the cows grazing in a pasture there. She promised that we would not go up to the top of the mountain, and that she would help me come back down the slope.

So, off I went, following my sister up the mountain. She was right in front of me, and I hurried along behind her in complete disregard for the fact that we were going UP the hillside because I trusted my big sister to take care of me.

About halfway up the mountain, we stopped to rest, and sat down on a large rock. That is when I first realized that I was halfway up the side of a huge mountain!

I looked back down the mountain path we had climbed, and sheer terror gripped my five-year-old heart. Frozen with fear, I could not speak or move. After a short rest, my sister jumped up and took off running up the mountain. "Come on, Linda. Let's go," she called.

But I could not respond. I just sat there on the rock, trying hard not to cry. When I did not stand up to follow her, Sue left me sitting on the rock and continued to follow the path up the mountain. I watched until she was out of sight, then wrapped my arms around my knees, and waited for her to return.

Sometime later that afternoon, Sue came skipping back to where she left me. "I'm ready to go back to the house now. Follow me back down the path." But I just sat there paralyzed. Fear had totally engulfed me, and I no longer trusted my sister to guide me safely down the mountain, or to catch me if I stumbled, because she had left me alone before.

After trying to convince me that there was nothing to fear, Sue gave up, and went down the mountain, leaving me there, sitting on a rock.

I do not know how long I sat there, but I do remember how afraid I was. The sun was beginning to set, the mountain air was getting cooler, and the echoes from the mountain valley below added to my fear.

Then, in the distance, I heard my mother calling my name. I was so relieved to see her walking toward me up the side of the mountain. I instinctively knew that I was safe, and that my mother would take care of me.

Lessons From The Purple Tree

So, I jumped up off the rock and began running down the mountain toward her. She took my hand, and led me the rest of the way home.

It was years later before I realized that my mother did not come all the way up the mountain to where I was sitting on the rock. I saw her on the path, and I left the rock and ran down the mountain.

It was total, unconditional trust that allowed me to take that first step. I trusted my mother to keep me safe; therefore, I was able to overcome my fear, and go down the mountain.

Trust was the belief that my mother truly cared for me, and that I could rely on her to guide me safely home.

In the workplace, trust is the belief that employees can believe in, and depend on, their managers and leaders. Trust is the assurance that
leaders are truly concerned with employee welfare, and the confidence that managers will deal fairly and honestly with everyone.

Trust removes doubt that leaders will not live up to their commitments to the workforce.

Leaders instill this trust in employees by treating people with a high degree of respect. It is the respect and value placed on people that allows them to contribute to the overall success of the company.

Trust allows companies and employees to work together, try new ideas and strategies, show initiative, and resolve conflict honorably. In turn, employees show trust to each other, and can build strong, cooperative teams.

Managers must prove their trustworthiness to the workforce. Regrettably, many managers play office favorites, and destroy workplace trust. The lack of trust is a huge barrier to good performance.

This can be avoided if managers make every effort to avoiding office politics, create positive work relationships, and seriously design a work environment that enhances rather than decreases employee morale.

Trust is the basic belief in integrity, and is based on consistency. Trust opens the door to change, and helps people accept change. It allows employees to do their best work and pay attention to the goals of the company, as well as their personal career aspirations.

Trust, the most critical component in an organization, is slowly built, but can be destroyed in a second. It is obvious when trust is broken, or begins to weaken.

Things that destroy trust are:

- Broken Promises
- Lack of confidentiality
- Falsifying information
- Lack of diversity
- Harassment (racial, gender, or general)

A work environment built on trust provides a culture and atmosphere free of harassment and discrimination, where people feel comfortable coming to work. It enables even the poorest performer to make improvements, and enhance their self-esteem.

Trust in the workplace begins at the leadership level, with fair policies, consistently and equitably applied, to all employees.

Managers and employees must spend time together finding ways to build and enhance trust, and understanding the pitfalls that can erode this hard-earned foundation of successful companies.

Lessons From The Purple Tree

Leaders can start the trust-building process by overcoming the barriers to trust within their organizations. This will allow employees to freely express their opinions and ideas without fear of reprisal.

Human beings need to feel good about themselves and feel connected and accepted at work. Feeling valued impacts the sense of trust within the company.

Another aspect of the trust issue is confidentiality. Violating a confidence, or spreading gossip about others, is a sure way to eliminate trust from the workplace.

Trust is built through repeated positive interactions with other people. Time spent on building trust at work will enhance opportunities for open communication.

It takes a high level of leadership ability to build trust in an organization. Listed below are a few steps to begin the process:

1. *Treat people with respect.* Automatically assume and believe that all employees want to do a good job, and treat each individual with respect, justice, and honesty.
2. *Implement policies fairly.* Make policy decisions that do not target or diminish the self-value of employees.
3. *Practice active listening, and learn to communicate well.* Share thoughts, feelings, and rational with others in the company, and allow employees to honestly express their opinions without fear of reprisal.
4. *Maintain a positive, upbeat attitude.* When employees observe managers resolve problems with a positive, pro-active attitude, they will feel

secure, and be more willing to participate in resolving workplace conflict.

5. *Say you are sorry when you make a mistake.* Nothing kills trust faster than leaders who refuse to accept accountability for their own actions.
6. *Practice solving problems without assigning blame.* Rather than trying to determine who is at fault, focus on how to resolve the problem. Turn these situations into opportunities to improve processes rather than 'pointing the finger of blame' at someone else.

Lessons From The Purple Tree

Manager Self-Check List

Place a check beside the statements
that apply to you:

- ❏ __I treat people with Respect
- ❏ __I am sincerely concerned about the welfare of my employees
- ❏ __I try hard to deal fairly and honestly with each individual
- ❏ __I live up to my commitments
- ❏ __I value the diversity in my workforce
- ❏ __I have zero-tolerance for workplace harassment
- ❏ __I do not have office favorites
- ❏ __I do not play office politics
- ❏ __I maintain a positive attitude
- ❏ __I practice solving problems without placing blame on others
- ❏ __I encourage employees to show initiative
- ❏ __I am consistent in administering corporate policies
- ❏ __I keep employee information confidential

Vision, Mission, and Goals

Growing up, our home was full of art, music, good food, and children. There were only four children in my immediately family; however, our home was the daily meeting place for every kid in the neighborhood. On any given day, there were a variety of children, of all ages, in the house, in the yard, or somewhere nearby.

My mother was quite happy with this arrangement, and spent many hours playing games, baking cookies, and watching children. She preferred to have her children at home so that she could keep an eye on us; thereby, by default, she became the neighborhood mother.

She did not discriminate in whether the child belonged to her or another parent, and she did not play favorites. Everyone was welcome, and my mother's home was a warm, loving haven for many boys and girls.

She instilled in each child the desire to be the best, and all the children adored my Mom because she treated each one special. She knew their names; she took the time to admire their 'mud pies' or the way they hit the baseball. She was connected, informed, and aware. All the neighborhood children felt included, and welcome.

Mother's artistic ability went far beyond canvas. She viewed everything, and **everyone**, as a potential masterpiece. Therefore, there was creativity flowing from every corner of our small house.

One day, a group of small children sat in a semi-circle on the living room floor, and watched as my mother painted a delightful beach scene. They were captivated by the vision coming to life before their very eyes!

As she painted, my mother talked to the children about the beauty of God's creation, and the opportunities for everyone who would accept the vision and reality of God's love.

You see, my mother was not using the traditional method of canvas and oil paint. She was painting directly on the living room wall! Over the course of a few days, she created a Seaside Mural that stretched the entire height and width of one wall.

The sweeping brush strokes applied directly on the plaster walls created a texture unmatched by artificial means. When finished, the beach scene was so realistic, that you could imagine the sounds of the ocean roar and feel the sunshine on your face.

Years later, I asked my Mother why she painted the mural on the wall. Her very candid response was, "I had a picture in my mind that was too large to put on a small canvas. I wanted to share that picture with everyone so they could clearly experience and understand it."

" I wanted to be able to see it everyday. If I had painted a traditional picture, I would have sold it or given it away, and only a few people would ever experience my vision. I put it on the wall so that everyone could enjoy it."

That powerful statement is appropriate for every boardroom, every director, every leader, in any size company or organization.

Put the vision where all can see it. Make it large, yet simple, so that employees can experience it. Make it bold and so impressive that it immediately catches the attention and admiration of the every individual.

When my mother is preparing to hang a painting in a gallery, or on the wall of her home, she is very careful to hang it in the exact right place. She is precise in measuring and plotting in order to ensure the picture is centered on the wall.

My mother says, "Hang the picture at eye level. Many artists make the mistake of hanging the picture too high on the wall, which forces people to 'look up' to see the painting. If you want the viewer to get the full picture, hang it at eye level."

Leaders could *take a good lesson* from her words. Many companies make the mistake of having a vision or mission statement that is hanging 'too high on the wall', and employees do not get the full impact of the purpose.

A well-defined company purpose gives employees direction and common goals. It provides focus in order to concentrate their work efforts appropriately, and allows them to use their time effectively.

If there is uncertainty about the meaning or purpose of the mission statement, employees might not be able to meet their goals. They may be unsure of how their specific job assignments support the overall mission of the company.

If written with simple language, there is no room for misunderstanding. All company and employee initiatives and goals can be measured against the mission statement, providing clear accountability and responsibility.

Employees should also be encouraged to write their own mission statement, describing their personal and professional ambitions and goals.

This is a good way for managers to find out where the employee's interests lie, how they want to grow their skills and career, and how they plan to make it happen. It will also provide the manager with insight into the values and potential concerns of the employee, and enable the manager to coach the employee more effectively.

In additional to personal mission statements, individuals who work in a team environment might consider writing a team mission statement that captures the needs, values, and beliefs of all the individuals on the team. Once in place, the team statement becomes the 'ruler' by which goals, actions, and accountabilities are measured.

Working together on this project will encourage open, honest, and direct communication between team members, and will motivate the team to better performance. The statement will also enforce the structure of the team and the role each team member plays.

Just as my mother gathered all the neighborhood children into her home, and made them feel welcome and included, managers should gather employees together and explain the vision of the company. Being available to answer questions, and observe employee reactions will allow spontaneous learning and improved teamwork.

Mother shared her artistic and spiritual vision with everyone, and was the motivation for many children becoming successful adults. A good leader will strive to instill that same motivation into the workforce, and be the catalyst that sparks action in others.

Manager Self-Check List

Place a check beside the statements that apply to you:

- ___Our company mission statement is clear and direct
- ___Every employee understands how their works supports the company goals
- ___I encourage employees to pursue their personal and professional goals
- ___I understand the values and concerns of my employees

Communication

Good Communication opens lines of knowledge, understanding, creativity, issue resolution, and agreement. It encourages cooperation among employees, and may reduce the possibility of unwanted turnover by promoting continuity of service. It also helps prevent conflicts.

Communication is critical to high performance and employee morale. The more frequently employees communicate, the more likely they will perform well.

In this highly technical age, the avenues and methods of communication are quite broad. It takes the form of letters, memos, e-mail, voice mail, tele-conferencing, and global interfacing, as well as face-to-face communication methods.

Even dissatisfied employees will work harder and better to meet company goals, if they are given an opportunity to communicate their thoughts and feelings.

Trust is a prerequisite to good communication. When employees do not trust their manager or co-workers, they are usually unwilling to communicate with them.

When people stop communicating with each other, it may be the result of lack of trust. This causes negative consequences such as confusion, tension, reduced productivity, resentment, frustration, and the inability of employees to do their jobs effectively.

When communication is conducted effectively, employees feel respected, valued, and trusted. They are free to express their own ideas openly and constructively.

An important aspect of whether or not people are willing to communicate is how managers respond when employees try to communicate.

Often, the actual words that are spoken are manipulated in a manner to hide the true feelings and intent. The Passive/Aggressive communication style can create tremendous confusion in the company, and will result in people feeling used, unappreciated, undervalued, and lacking self-value.

Nonverbal communication often discloses what the spoken word does not say. Body language, eye contact, gestures, and personal space requirements may enlighten managers as to the true feelings of the employees.

Several behaviors tend to stop good communication:

- Judging
- Superiority
- Controlling
- Manipulation
- Indifference

In addition to the actual spoken words, inappropriate tone of voice and body language can stop good communication.

Effective listening skills are essential in communicating with employees and managers. Nonverbal examples of active listening include simple actions such as:

- Leaning forward
- Smiling
- Nodding
- Eye contact
- Paying full attention

Communication will certainly come to a fast stop when behaviors, such as superiority or judging others, exist. Employees will be offended, and will react defensively.

The consequences will be that they are reluctant to offer ideas, become quiet, refrain from asking questions, and will not admit to mistakes.

There must be a connection between both parties of the exchange, with ideas and information openly and respectfully shared, in order for communication in a company to be effective.

The Power of Listening

One of the most important factors determining success in the workplace is the ability of people to listen to each other.

This skill supports all the other activities that define an organization's ability to survive in today's competitive environment.

While everyone agrees that listening skills are important, it is one area that gets very little attention. Few companies offer training to develop listening capacity in employees.

Throughout my childhood, and even as an adult, I have been told to "listen". Schoolteachers, parents, and every level of the corporate hierarchy assume that if an individual has the physical ability to 'hear', they have active listening skills by default.

Sporadic training is administered in the workplace to help employees understand the concepts and power of active listening.

Likewise, some school systems are making the same assumptions with students, and perhaps have below-average performance due to inadequate or untaught listening skills at all levels.

Listening well is the ability to be attentive, and absorb what is being said, while reserving judgment. People can process words spoken by others much faster than they can speak themselves.

Most people speak comfortably at a rate of approximately 125 words per minute. The average person can actually listen to approximately 418 words per minute; however, they can think more than 2,000 words per minute.

This leaves a great deal of time to analyze and evaluate what the speaker is saying. This extra time can be a disadvantage since individuals tend to concentrate only minimally on what is being said, and their minds wander off to other topics of interest.

An important listening skill is nonverbal listening. In its most basic form, this includes reacting non-verbally by nodding, maintaining eye contact, and leaning forward.

Another tactic of active listening is paraphrasing expressed facts and feelings. Sometimes called reflecting, the response begins with, "Let me make sure I understand what you said. Did I understand you to say..."

The goal of paraphrasing is to make sure there is clarity about what the speaker intended, and to let the speaker know the listener cares about what they are saying.

The techniques of active listening are strong tools for helping employees find the right words to express their thoughts or feelings and to maximize their contributions to the company.

Active listening helps individuals develop self-understanding. In the process of explaining how they feel, and explaining their thoughts, employees often come to a better understanding of the issue.

Leaders who possess the ability to listen well will create purpose and commitment within the workforce. Employees will feel appreciated, and their self-esteem will be heightened when a manager expresses true understanding by practicing active listening.

Linda F. Felker, Ph.D.

Manager Self-Check List

Place a check beside the statements
that apply to you:

- ❒ __I maintain effective communication with my employees
- ❒ __My communication is not passive-aggressive
- ❒ __I do not practice controlling or manipulative methods in my communication
- ❒ __I use active listening skills
- ❒ __I listen carefully to what the employee is saying, reserving judgement.
- ❒ __I enhance my employees self-esteem by with my communication methods

Feedback

One of the household tasks that I do well is sweeping the kitchen floor. I am quite proud of this accomplishment, not because of the resulting clean floor, but because of the *way I learned to sweep the floor.*

My mother was a firm believer in assigning household chores to her children. She believed in "train up a child in the way he should go", and wanted all her children to be self-sufficient adults.

She taught me all the normal household tasks, including cooking, making beds, laundry, washing dishes, and sweeping the kitchen floor.

Mother didn't wait until I was a teenager to begin the training. She started young. At a very young age, my daily task was to sweep the kitchen floor each night after supper.

The broom was long-handled, and quite large. I was short, and sometimes had difficulty holding the broom. However, that was my assigned chore, and I did it happily.

But, I did not do it well. I swept to what I thought was the best of my ability, and then mother would come and inspect my work. She always told me what I did right; then, would point out one or two areas that I did not do well. I was required to go back and do it again, until I swept the floor to her satisfaction.

There were many nights when I swept that floor four or five times. But, the way she delivered the feedback to me was so positive, and encouraging, that I tried my hardest to sweep the floor just to make my mother proud.

Of course, I am sure it would have been so much easier for her to do the work herself. In a matter of a few minutes, she could have swept the floor, and not had to coach me for thirty minutes to get it right.

Had she taken that approach, I probably would have relied on her to assume my responsibilities in other areas of my life. My mother provided support and feedback, but did not remove responsibility for the task itself.

Leaders can have the same impact on employees if they are giving feedback in the right way that encourages employees to improve their work and strive for superior performance.

The problem many employees face is that the feedback they receive falls in the category of "too little, too late", or not at all.

Inadequate feedback will make employees feel unsure about their performance, and de-motivated. It can lead to failure. Appropriate feedback builds
employees confident, accelerates the level of trust in those giving the feedback, guides people in the right direction, and sets individuals up for success.

Feedback helps people achieve peak performance, and encourages them to repeat prior good performance. It helps people learn.

Feedback benefits the leader by building a group of skilled, knowledgeable workers who can work more independently. An effective, self-directed group of employees allows the manager to focus more time on other leadership activities.

Feedback benefits the organization because it creates an environment where people willing ask for and provide suggestions, trust others to be honest and supportive, and are encouraged to enhance and improve performance.

There are two types of feedback: praise, or positive feedback, and corrective feedback.

Effective feedback balances positive feedback and praise with corrective feedback. Positive feedback lets employees know that they are doing well, and clearly states the actions and behaviors that are correct. Corrective feedback lets people know which performance areas need to be enhanced, changed, or improved.

Balanced feedback maintains employee self-esteem. In order to provide these types of feedback, the manager should know exactly what the employee did well, realize how they accomplished the goal, and be prepared to discuss suggestions for continued improvement.

Most managers do not enjoy giving corrective feedback; however, this type of feedback is necessary to allow people an opportunity to adjust their performance to the levels needed by the company to ensure success.

If given in the right way, employees will not react negatively to corrective feedback; they will find the feedback helpful.

It is also important that feedback be given at the proper time. When someone makes a mistake, the manager should not hesitate to initiate the feedback discussion. Delaying feedback could cause the employee to feel embarrassed, angry, or insulted. Plus, the feedback might be useless if the discussion happens long after the event.

The wise manager will not only give feedback to employees, but also actively solicit feedback on their own performance regularly. If an atmosphere of trust is established, employees will feel comfortable providing their manager with specific feedback, and offering suggestions to the manager that will help improve communication, team alignment, managerial quality, and overall performance.

Using a 360 Feedback tool is usually quite helpful to leaders, and identifies areas where employees are satisfied, as well as potential problematic situations. Being proactive in resolving the problem areas will enhance employee morale, improve overall employee performance, and ensure company strategic goals and plans are met.

Manager Self-Check List

Place a check beside the statements
that apply to you:

- ___My goal in providing feedback is to help employees improve their performance
- ___My feedback is always balanced
- ___My feedback is always timely
- ___I provide specific details of the situation when providing feedback
- ___I build trust and confidence with employees during feedback meetings
- ___I create an environment where people are willing for ask for help
- ___My employees trust me to give fair feedback
- ___I maintain or enhance the employees' self-esteem during feedback conversations
- ___I solicit feedback from employees on my performance as a manager

Commitment

"Mama, do you see that doll in the store window? She is so beautiful! Will you buy her for me, mama? Will you, *please*?"

Mother put her arm around my shoulder, and guided me into the store to get a closer look at the doll. She lifted the doll off the shelf, and placed her gently in my outstretched arms. The doll was about 12 inches tall, and made entirely of hard plastic. Even her hair was molded plastic. Her only clothing was a cotton shirt and a diaper.

I hugged the doll close to my face, and breathed in the 'smell'. To me, that plastic smell was intoxicating, and that doll was the most beautiful doll I had ever seen.

I wanted that doll, and asked my mother again, "Will you buy her for me, mama. I'll take good care of her, I promise!" Mother took the doll and put her back up on the high shelf. Then she took me by the hand and walked toward the door.

"I cannot buy that doll for you, honey," she explained. "It is not your birthday, and Christmas is still a long way off. If we go home and your brothers and sister see that I bought you a doll, and did not buy them anything, it will hurt their feelings. I don't have enough money to buy a gift for everyone today."

I knew my mother was right. My family was rich in blessings, but very little money was available for extra things. Still, I really wanted that doll.

"But mama, I will help pay for the doll. See, I have money," I pleaded. Stopping on the sidewalk, I opened my small purse, and showed my mother the change I had saved.

Mother reached into the purse and counted the change. "That is only 50 cents, Linda. The doll costs much more than that. If you really want that doll, you will need to save the money yourself," said mother.

All the way home, I thought about what my mother said. How could I possibly save that much money? At eight years old, the only money I received was school lunch money. My mind whirled as I calculated and planned. I would save all the money my parents gave me to buy my lunch at school! Soon, I would have enough money to buy the doll.

The next morning, as my mother was in her room getting dressed for work, I slipped into the kitchen
and made a peanut butter sandwich, and carefully wrapped it in a napkin. When mother gave me lunch money, I put it in my little purse.

That day at school, I sat at a table in the lunchroom and ate my peanut butter sandwich, washed down with water from the fountain.

Each day for weeks, I followed the same plan. I ate a sandwich and drank water in order to save my money. Every night, I counted the growing pile of coins in my little purse. At the end of three weeks, I had saved enough money to buy the doll.

Lessons From The Purple Tree

"Mama, will you take me shopping tomorrow? I want to buy that doll we saw a few weeks ago at the toy store." Mother looked surprised, and said," Sweetheart, I explained to you that I cannot buy that doll for you right now. As much as I would enjoy giving it to you, I do not have extra money right now. You just have to understand."

"But mama, you don't understand. I saved the money myself, just like you said. Look!" I held out the open purse and proudly displayed all the money I saved.

"Where did you get all this change?" mother asked. As I explained to her how I decided on a plan, and saved my lunch money, a big smile came across my mother's face.

She grabbed me up in a tight hug, and spoke softly in my ear. "Linda, I am so proud of you for finding a way to save the money yourself. Although I wish you had not deprived yourself of a hot, nourishing lunch, you did a great job in creating a plan and following it through."

The feeling of accomplishment and joy I felt when I presented my purse full of change to the clerk at the toy store enhanced my self-confidence and pride. I was committed to fulfilling my dream, and mother was committed to supporting me in the achievement.

This lesson is applicable to all levels in the workforce. High levels of employee commitment will largely determine the effectiveness and success of the company. If individuals are going to implement plans and follow through on assignments, they must be committed to the organization.

When employees know that the company is committed to providing an environment that values diversity, provides growth, offers enrichment opportunities, and supports initiative, they will obtain what they need and want from the company. In addition, the company will have the potential for economic gain.

This commitment creates an excitement and satisfaction in individual job assignments and enhances self-esteem, as well as feelings of significance among team members.

Committed employees will not say, "That's not my job" when asked to help others. Instead, they willingly and voluntarily realize that they have an obligation to assist others and do more than is stated in their official job description.

Corporate leaders must figure out that loyalty is earned, and is well defined and established at the top organizational levels. Managers must ensure that their actions clearly support their commitment to employees, and their desire to establish a work environment that demonstrates that same commitment appropriately.

A good leader understands what people need, and knows that workers appreciate a meaningful, intellectual, and emotional connection between themselves, the work, their co-workers, the manager, and the workplace.

Employees want a culture that offers external rewards, but also offers the satisfaction that comes from doing challenging work. The benefit of this strategy is that people will want to stay, and give more of their head and hearts to their work.

Identifying and implementing effective employee retention and satisfaction strategies will help ensure an environment that is more efficient and profitable.

Employee stress is a major contributor to workplace hazard. One in five workers suffers from high levels of work-related stress, with over 500,000 individuals experiencing illness directly related to stress. Research links stress to high turnover and high levels of sickness absence. Furthermore, companies are losing sales because of the high stress levels of their workforce.

While fair compensation and opportunities to advance are always important factors, most people decide to leave a company because of their personal opinion of their direct manager. Commitment to the company, and length of an employee's stay, is determined largely by whether or not the manager has established a positive, respectful work relationship with the employee.

Leaders must accept accountability for employee satisfaction, and be committed to retention strategies designed to engage, satisfy, and retain workers. Although salary and benefits are part of the total picture, employees appreciate the chance to be heard and make decisions regarding their work.

Most workers do not really want to leave their jobs, but feel they must leave to achieve certain personal satisfaction.

The top four reasons why employees voluntarily leave a company are:

1. *Lack of confidence in their manager or the company* When an employee loses confidence and hope, he or she may consider changing jobs.
2. *Lack of recognition.* Workers need to be recognized, rewarded, and developed. Exiting employees often cite lack of recognition, inadequate rewards, and too little opportunity to build on their personal abilities as reasons for leaving. When employers are not committed to fulfilling these needs, the employee concludes that there are no other available options but to leave.
3. *Lack of trust.* Too many broken promises and commitments not kept are a significant problem in the

workplace. If employees feel the company is not loyal to them, they will not be committed to high-performance and continuity. A broken promise or lack of management commitment destroys trust.
4. *Lack of communication and listening.* Employees need to believe they are being heard. If managers fail to listen to the needs of employees, workers may feel undervalued.

Organizations should conduct an in-depth analysis of employee turnover and understand why good people leave. If poor manager quality is driving turnover, it is imperative that immediate and significant changes occur.

When workers realize that managers are truly interested and committed to their well being, they are more likely to reevaluate their reasons for leaving. Managers can enhance their commitment to employees by:

- Being connected to individuals
- Understanding how the work is done
- Offering support and information
- Helping with difficult projects
- Linking the employee's work to company objectives
- Effective coaching and feedback
- Listening and responding empathetically to worker concerns

Moreover, leaders who consistently display appreciation, and generate enthusiasm and excitement within the team, are rewarded with more dedicated and loyal workers.

Organizations must have the desire to create a cohesive, committed, all-for-one workplace culture. It takes great people to build a great company; therefore, significant effort must be put into employee retention strategies to retain top talent.

My mother showed her commitment to me by thoroughly explaining the situation, offering a suggestion, and then stepping back and allowing me to think of my own solution.

She was not pleased with the fact that I forfeited a good, nutrition lunch in order to buy a doll; however, she was pleased that I made a plan and followed it through.

Mother provided an atmosphere in which she allowed us to make mistakes, and learn from them. And, she provided praise for our efforts. I never doubted my mother's commitment to me. She inspired me to display that same level of commitment to my own children and family.

Linda F. Felker, Ph.D.

Manager Self-Check List

Place a check beside the statements that apply to you

- ☐ ___I am committed to my employees
- ☐ ___My employees know I am committed to them
- ☐ ___I promote a safe environment for people to work
- ☐ ___I allow workers to learn from their mistakes
- ☐ ___I provide appropriate praise and reinforcement
- ☐ ___I am committed to creating a cohesive, cooperative corporate culture
- ☐ ___I am committed to understanding work process
- ☐ ___I find creative ways to recognize my employees

Lessons From The Purple Tree

"A great leader is someone who has the ability to get other people to do what they don't want to do, and like it."
Harry Truman

"You do not lead by hitting people over the head. That's assault, not leadership"
D. D. Eisenhower

The Leadership Challenge

Leadership is the ability to influence others to achieve successful results. That sounds very simple. However, the ability to lead others, and do it well, is not a simple task.

Today's managers must have the leadership qualities and skills that will help them successfully manage a diverse group of employees. They must be able to monitor the changes taking place in the economy as well as in customer trends, and make adjustments according to corporate strategy. They must be able to produce high results, yet still meet the needs of employees, senior leadership, shareholders, and customers.

Time constraints and working with others is a challenge. At a minimum, customer demands *must* be satisfied, deadlines *must* be met, and results *must* meet and/or exceed company goals and expectations.

Leaders must be able to make sound and fair decisions, provide feedback and advice as they structure employee work assignments, and
encourage employees to grow and develop personally and professionally.

It is important for workers at every level of the business to understand the corporate mission and vision, and know how their work helps meet the company goals.

Individual goals must be set and leaders must empower others to be successful while complying with high-level corporate plans and initiatives.

If a leader does not possess the fundamental skill and ability to motivate employees, then there is a good probability that frustration and conflict will occur in the workplace.

The ability to build and sustain trusting, positive relationships is crucial to any successful manager. However, understanding how to accomplish this continues to be a problem to many leaders.

Survival for many companies and employees depends on finding ways to establish positive relationships with customers and suppliers, as well as with internal and work partners.

Creating synergy between company departments and teams will prepare the group for greater accomplishments and success in a global environment that is constantly changing.

Today's workers no longer just "show up for work". They are expected to demonstrate passion and purpose in the workplace, and plug into their creative toolbox to make process improvement suggestions.

There has been a dramatic increase in the use of employees, their ideas, and their suggestions. Encouraging workers to high levels of creativity and innovation is the responsibility of the leader.

Due to the past decade of downsizing, restructuring, and economies of scale in the corporate environment, employees may have fewer opportunities for advancement into management or supervisory positions. This situation requires the manager to search for other opportunities to empower workers, and allow them the freedom to make decisions that impact their work.

An empowered worker will have the confidence and ability to manage their own daily work assignments, and become an asset to the manager, the team, and the company.

The successful leader must be able to coach, provide meaningful feedback to others to enable top performance, meet strategic goals, and continue to provide cross-training and other developmental opportunities for the workforce at large.

Given the decrease in advancement opportunities available to employees, the right motivators should be incorporated to keep the workforce committed and performing at high levels. Employees must be made to feel valued, understood, and appreciated for the contributions they make everyday.

There are tremendous competitive demands on companies, which result in pressure to obtain maximum productivity from every employee.

Employees will have more responsibility with no additional resources; however, if managers honestly convey the challenge to employees in a positive way, are able to answer questions, and assist with change management, it will help create an environment where employees feel they are important. They will have an increased desire to give 100% of their talent and abilities, and will actively look for ways they can contribute to the success of their company,

True leadership from company managers is essential in ensuring corporate success, reducing unnecessary turnover, and motivating individuals to be more productive. Organizations must establish a great plan for success, and provide capable leadership to encourage employees to grow and develop their capabilities, both professionally and personally.

Benefits to the manager who actively motivates employees:

- Higher productivity
- Deadlines met
- Work more satisfying and enjoyable
- Skills fully developed and used
- Problems solved; crisis avoided
- Quality increased to satisfy customers

All of these are good reasons for learning and using the leadership skills that will produce a positive work environment. Moreover, leaders and employees must be able to work together to:

- Offer thoughtful suggestions, and creative solutions to employee issues and concerns
- Implement work plans and company strategies fairly and consistently across the organization
- Ensure they are acting with integrity, building trust, and conducting business ethically

Building trust is vital, and critical to the success of any company, and is a significant factor in whether the organization will achieve success.

The leader who can build trust within the workforce will avoid many of the pitfalls and problems that come with managing people.

Leaders are in a powerful position, and make significant contributions into how people feel about their jobs.

The number one reason people say they quit their jobs is their immediate manager. The number one reason people say they stay and like their jobs is their immediate manager.

If a leader does not have good, solid working relationships with the people who are actually doing the work, the leader will not earn their respect, loyalty, or cooperation. It is a major mistake for managers to only work to establish their employees' 'head knowledge' and neglect the importance of connecting with their 'heart knowledge'; they will not
have the full commitment and willingness to contribute from the workforce.

Workers will not be as likely to give 100 percent to the job, which could result in unmet goals, declining productivity, and diminished quality. Bottom line - it means the leader is not effective.

Good leaders are the foundation of a company's success. They are the link to the frontline employees, and their ability to maximizing performance and increase profit.

The quality leader is crucial to identifying, hiring and retaining the best employees, and the primary reason employees give the extra effort and passion to their jobs.

Almost any leader can get people to do enough to keep their positions and paychecks. The outstanding leader has the ability to motivate and influence employees to give more than is required, and do the job well.

For the past 20 years, I have worked within the corporate structure to facilitate change, and develop quality leaders. I have enjoyed the unique opportunity to provide enrichment, growth, and training to leaders at every level of the corporate hierarchy.

The primary concern in most organizations continues to be employee performance and employee retention. These two issues directly impact bottom line profitability. Solving these problems is not easy. I have seen senior management search for hard answers and implement solutions that should have been successful. But, they were not successful.

The main reason these interventions failed was that employees did not have trust in the company or in their leadership team.

Employees did not feel they were not involved in the solution; therefore, they were not committed to the result. And, employees did not feel respected and valued at work. Without trust, there can be no lasting solution to creating a safe environment for employees to learn, make mistakes, improve their performance, and, thereby, retain good talent.

The simple, storybook method used in "Lessons From The Purple Tree" is intended to highlight five leadership competencies that are critical to overall corporate success.

Of course, there are many competencies and abilities that must be inherent in any successful company. The five discussed in this book are the foundation.

The lessons explained in these chapters translate to the boardroom and the frontline.

There is wisdom be gained by learning "through the eyes of a child". Likewise, there is enormous wisdom to be learned through the insight of a Godly Mother.

God Bless You as you select the vibrant colors of your own "Purple Tree".

Lessons From The Purple Tree

Manager Self-Check List

Place a check beside the statements
that apply to you:

- ❐ ___I influence others to achieve success
- ❐ ___I have the leadership skills necessary to manage a diverse group of employees
- ❐ ___I produce high results, while meeting the needs of employees and customers
- ❐ ___I make sound and fair decisions
- ❐ ___My employees understand the importance of our corporate mission and vision
- ❐ ___I empower others to be successful
- ❐ ___I build and sustain positive relationships
- ❐ ___I create synergy between company departments and teams
- ❐ ___I provide effective coaching for employees to enable them to meet their goals
- ❐ ___I motivate others to be successful
- ❐ ___I offer thoughtful suggestions and solutions to employee issues and concerns
- ❐ ___I act with Integrity, Build Trust, and am Ethical in business situations

Acknowledgements

This work would not have been possible without the prayerful support of many people. My mother's faith in me was the spark that enabled me to reach for my dreams. Her enthusiasm is contagious. My husband provided unselfish support that allowed me to concentrate my attention to the accomplishment of this goal.

Many people throughout the years have encouraged me to write this book. Often, during seminars and workshops, I related a personal story to reinforce the objective of the training. This book represents a few of those stories.

Love to all my family, especially Todd, Marci, Brent, Zachary, Jackson, Ann, Sue, Clark, Joey, Ellen, Susan, Roy, Mary Clare, Stephen, Amy, and Joseph. To my special aunt, Lona Henderson, thank you for always being there for me. And, thanks to my father, Joseph Fox, Sr., for the music in my life.

Above all, I thank God for his love, mercy, and abundant blessings.

References

Corporate Leadership Council, Corporate Executive Board, 1998. New Tools for Managing Workforce Stability and Engagement

Felker, L. F., 2004. The Impact of Management Psychological Behaviors on Call Center Employee Retention.

Printed in the United States
19392LVS00001B/142-243